Praises for The Gratitude Attitude

Although I was familiar with some of Newell's 'nuggets,' it took me six years in a North Vietnamese POW camp to *really* understand and appreciate their value. Take my advice: Read, enjoy, and digest this book and you'll have knowledge I had to learn the hard way!

—Captain J. Charles (Charlie) Plumb, USN (Retired)
Author of *I'm No Hero* and www.CharliePlumb.com

The Gratitude Attitude is a timely book for the person seeking to understand why so many in contemporary American society are apathetic toward the feelings and well-being of others. While expanding the reader's understanding, Newell motivates him to a higher level by providing a unique journaling method to develop his capacity for living a more meaningful life. *The Gratitude Attitude* should find itself on everyone's bookshelf!

—Dr. Tom Gaines, CEO
The Institute for Leadership and Ethics, Inc.

the
Gratitude
Attitude

by J. Carl Newell

TATE PUBLISHING & *Enterprises*

Published by Tate Publishing & Enterprises, LLC
127 E. Trade Center Terrace | Mustang, Oklahoma 73064 USA
1.888.361.9473 | www.tatepublishing.com

Tate Publishing is committed to excellence in the publishing industry. The company reflects the philosophy established by the founders, based on Psalm 68:11,
"The Lord gave the word and great was the company of those who published it."

Book design copyright © 2007 by Tate Publishing, LLC. All rights reserved.
Cover design by Geneveive Stotler
Interior design by Lindsay B. Behrens

Published in the United States of America

ISBN: 978-1-60462-113-6
1. Inspiration   2. Journals   3. Diaries   4. Devotionals
07.10.10

To Martha
My best friend
My consistent compass
My wife

Acknowledgment

It is with deep gratitude and heartfelt admiration and appreciation that I acknowledge the immeasurable contributions made by our nation's military veterans to win and preserve our freedom.

Whether conscript or volunteer, every person who honorably served in the United States Army, Air Force, Coast Guard, Marine Corps, or Navy has made a meaningful contribution to ensuring safety and security for generations of Americans. Some were asked to give more and some less, but all played an essential role in making the USA the greatest nation on earth.

While most served a tour of duty and returned home unscathed and unscarred, millions were wounded or killed and still others spent thousands of days living in squalor and deprivation—often enduring torture—as a prisoner of war while serving our country.

Several years ago, the rear bumper of numerous automobiles displayed a bumper sticker with this thought-provoking message: "If you can read this, thank a teacher!"

Wouldn't it be a wonderful expression of appreciation to our veterans if every car in the USA honored them in a similar way? Maybe a bumper sticker that says...

"If you enjoy freedom and prosperity, thank a veteran!"

Thanks veterans...we owe you a huge debt of gratitude!

Contents

Foreword * 11

Introduction * 13

Change Your World * 17

Light Your Torch * 27

The Gratitude Attitude * 41

Learn to Live! * 161

End Notes * 185

About the Author * 191

Foreword

J. Carl Newell is a great American and a devoted Christian with a strong belief in God and in his country. The message in *The Gratitude Attitude* effectively communicates his concern for individuals and the future of our society.

God fully equipped us to enjoy life and experience satisfaction and fulfillment along the way. I believe that He is disappointed when we sit around and worry about things over which we have no control and fret about things within our control without taking action to change them. He wants us to choose to have a winner's attitude and to constantly be moving toward a more meaningful life.

Personal failures and successes are great teachers but the best—and least painful—way to learn valuable life lessons is from the experience of others. Many of my most valuable lessons were learned during my military service and as I traveled the world observing other peoples and societies. In combat, my faith in God grew, as did my respect for the words honor and gratitude.

I wish I could sit down at a campfire with all of America's young people and they would listen to my words of advice. They are simple words:

- No one is perfect, so treat everyone with dignity and respect.
- Never forget to show gratitude for the contributions of others toward your success.

This compelling book highlights these and other valuable lessons necessary for real success in life. It's an easy to read book that is hard to lay aside once you begin. The poems, Bible verses, and other nuggets of wisdom allow you to mentally relax with a suggestive power that engages your feelings and imagination with the true rhythm and meaning of life.

In my opinion, *The Gratitude Attitude* is truly "a gift within your grasp!"

—*1SG Nick D. Bacon, USA (Retired)*
Congressional Medal of Honor
President, DVC, Inc.
North Little Rock, AR

Introduction

This old world just ain't what it used to be!

There was a time when students and young couples looked toward the future without undue fear. Uncertainty? Yes. Trepidation? Perhaps. But near-paralyzing fear? No!

Young people growing-up in the 1950s, '60s, and '70s were accustomed to a society in which kindness, consideration, trust, and respect were implicit in relationships—both personal and business.

Looking back through the lens of five decades of history, the mores of the "baby boomer" generation seem to have been both simple and naive. But were they?

- Where is the naiveté in respecting a person's character?
- Where is the simplicity in accepting a person's word as a good faith promise?
- What's the problem with believing that a person will do what she says she will do?
- What factors have contributed to our society becoming increasingly distrustful—often to the point of paranoia—over the past few decades?

Middle-aged Americans experiencing the transition from a relatively simple and slow-paced *Leave It to Beaver* society to today's unrealistic Simpsonesque lifestyles are baffled, wondering, "How did it happen?"

My concern is not, "How did it happen?" but rather, "What are we going to do about it?" Personally, I have no problem with technologic microwaves, grandma traveling around the world at supersonic speeds, or kids carrying hand-held computers with the processing power of a 1980s IBM 360 mainframe computer.

My fear is that human beings—boys and girls and men and women of all ages—are missing out on some of life's richest blessings!

More than 150 years ago, Henry David Thoreau made this extraordinary observation: "Most men lead lives of quiet desperation and go to the grave with the song still in them."

Unfortunately, many of us will go to the grave in the twenty-first century without releasing our song because we don't understand the fundamentals of life. Setting-aside the complexities of sagging economies, depressed world markets, and the uncertainty of tomorrow, the average person doesn't seem to grasp the fact that success and happiness is up to the individual. *It's an inside job!*

Understanding the very basics essential for achieving a contented, satisfying, and enjoyable life filled with meaningful relationships seems to be lacking in the mind of the average American. Most are completely unaware of the immense power residing within them…the power to design and accomplish a truly remarkable life!

My goal in writing this book is to provide a practical and easy way for people to enrich their lives by applying this timeless truth: *It is more blessed to give than to receive!*

If this book helps just one person catch a glimpse of the immense joy and satisfaction awaiting them when an attitude of gratitude becomes personal habit, my objective will have been achieved.

—*J. Carl Newell*
Loganville, Georgia

How far you go in life depends on your being
tender with the young,
compassionate with the aged,
sympathetic with the striving,
and tolerant of the weak and the strong
because someday you will have been all of these.[1]

Change Your World

What the world needs now, is love, sweet love,
No, not just for some, but for everyone.[2]

Things that don't change tend to remain the same.

If the world needed love in the 1960s when Burt Bacharach and Hal David composed the hit song, *What the World Needs Now*, the entire universe must be clamoring for it now!

Love embodies much more than the erotic passion depicted by Hollywood moguls and popularized by the current television and print media. Genuine love was explicitly defined nearly 2000 years ago through the pen of the Apostle Paul:

> Love is patient, love is kind. It does not envy, it does not boast, it is not proud. It is not rude, it is not self-seeking, it is not easily angered, it keeps no record of wrongs. Love does not delight in evil but rejoices with the truth. It always protects, always trusts, always hopes, always perseveres. Love never fails...And now these three remain: faith, hope and love. But the greatest of these is love.
>
> —1 Corinthians 13:4–8a, 13

The compassionate attitude of mainstream America during the early twentieth century and through the Great Depression, sandwiched between two World Wars, resulted in neighbors voluntarily helping each other and even strangers have a better life. This behavioral pattern motivated by a common attitude has declined steadily over recent decades.

By 1952 the national mood had dramatically changed. When the question, "Are people as honest and moral as they used to be?" was included in a national survey, 47% responded, "Yes."

Fifty years later, when people were asked the same question, a whopping 73% answered, "No."[3]

Is it any wonder that many twenty-first century citizens are skeptical and suspicious to almost the point of paranoia when faced with acts of love disguised as gratitude and kindness?

What's Wrong with the World?

Global warming is an issue worrying many people and generating considerable national and international debate. While the earth's temperature continues to record minuscule increases year over year[4], global warming is not the gravest danger facing today's world.

Global *cooling* is a far greater threat to the survival of humankind than the prospects that civilization will someday suffocate due to mismanagement of its industrialization. While the developing greenhouse effect captures headlines, the insidious global cooling effect aggressively attacking the grassroots of society is largely ignored.

The core of this societal malignancy is unintentional, perhaps unrecognized, apathy. Many people simply do not see themselves as a significant part of society as a whole. By encapsulating their personal warmth, love, and compassion within their own small world, the rest of the world is given a benign, cold neglect.

Consistent increases in violent crime have actively personified Robert Burns' preview of "man's inhumanity to man."[5] When rapid and incessant change coupled with national turmoil and international instability are tossed into the mix, a host of non-specific fears are generated within us, fears that calcify our sensitivity. Our hearts are not as easily touched as in the past, and our optimism is flagging. At the same time our hopes for the future are fast fading.

The Cold Within

Six humans trapped by happenstance
In black and bitter cold,
Each one possessed a stick of wood,
Or so the story's told.

Their dying fire in need of logs,
The first woman held hers back;
For on the faces around the fire
She noticed one was black.

The next man looking across the way
Saw one not of his church,
And couldn't bring himself to give
The fire his stick of birch.

The third one sat in tattered clothes;
He gave his coat a hitch.
Why should his log be put to use
To warm the idle rich?

The rich man just sat back and thought
Of the wealth he had in store.
And how to keep what he had earned
From the lazy poor.

The black man's face bespoke revenge
As the fire passed from his sight,
For all he saw in his stick of wood
Was a chance to spite the white.

And the last man of this forlorn group
Did naught except for gain.
Giving only to those who gave
Was how he played the game.

The logs held tight in death's still hands
Was proof of human sin.
They didn't die from the cold without;
They died from the cold within.

—James Patrick Kinney[6]

This sad and distressing condition is a byproduct of rapid technological and societal change fused to an ever-increasing indifference in human relationships. Thus the quantity and quality of interpersonal interaction and non-threatening small group discussions appears to be deteriorating at a shocking rate.

I am absolutely convinced that every person's own small world—the composite of which makes up our civilization—would be wondrously expanded and enriched if everyone played the game of life fairly and by the rules.

The Game of Life

Life is sometimes referred to as a game. In a sense, this is a legitimate comparison because decisions made by players in an athletic contest create circumstances affecting the final outcome. Likewise, making wise choices daily and playing by the rules are strategic actions for becoming a winner in life.

Nearly 2000 years ago, Jesus—the Head Coach and life's Official Scorer—defined a crucial element for developing a winning game plan when He said: "So in everything, do to others what you would have them do to you, for this sums up the Law and the Prophets" (Matthew 7:12).

This pithy statement known as the Golden Rule is the foundational principle on which a life characterized by Christian love and compassion is built. To their credit, many other world religions have adopted a similar teaching:

Brahmanism: This is the sum of duty: do naught unto others which would cause you pain if done unto you.

Buddhism: Hurt not others in ways that you yourself would find hurtful.

Confucianism: Do not unto others what you would not have them do unto you.

Hindu: The true role in life is to guard and do by the things of others as they do on their own.

Islam: No one of you is a believer until he desires for his brother that which he desires for himself.

Judaism: Whatever is hurtful to yourself, do not to your fellowman. That is the whole of the law, the rest is merely commentary.

Persian: Do as you would be done by.

Taoism: Regard your neighbor's gain as your own gain and your neighbor's loss as your own loss.[7]

The bottom-line message is that life is all about relationships. When personal interactions are characterized by non-judgmental, considerate, and compassionate behavior, we are playing by the rules.

Life...It's All About Relationships

As insignificant as we may see ourselves, the fact is that each of us is an integral, interlocking piece of life's puzzle. John W. Gardner, the eminent educator and presidential advisor, describes the human condition this way:

It's interesting that we come to understand in early child-hood the impact various others have on us, but many of us are middle-aged before we begin to understand the impact we have on others—which is a pity because the impact you have on others may create the environment in which you live.[8]

Dr. Gardner's commentary lends credence to John Donne's observation that "no man is an island, entire of itself."[9] Since life is an incredible mixture of complex personal interactions, it is impossible to live in today's world without affecting other people. You must realize that your actions—or sometimes, inaction—affect your life *and* the lives of others.

Many psychologists share a conviction that human beings are more alike than different. Just as everyone needs oxygen, food, and water to survive and thrive in life, everyone needs to experience positive human interactions on a regular basis.

We must learn to recognize and respond to subtle, but very real, needs in the lives of people around us. The renowned American psychiatrist Dr. Karl Menninger explained our common malady like this:

When a trout rising to a fly gets hooked and finds himself unable to swim about freely, he begins a fight which results in struggles and splashes and sometimes an escape…In the same way, the human being struggles…with the hooks that catch him. Sometimes he masters his difficulties; sometimes they are too much for him. His struggles are all that the world sees, and it usually misunderstands them. It is hard for a free fish to understand what is happening to a hooked one.[10]

If indeed we're more alike than different and if the impact we have on others can improve our society, doesn't it make sense that we strive to be more thoughtful, patient, and considerate in our personal interactions?

The quality of your life depends
on the quality of your relationships.
The quality of your relationships depends
on you...and how you play the game!

For when the One Great Scorer comes
To write against your name,
He marks—not that you won or lost—
But how you played the game."

I'd rather be ashes than dust.
I would rather that my spark would burn out
in a brilliant blaze than be stifled by dry rot.
I would rather be a superb meteor,
every atom of me in magnificent glow,
than a sleepy and permanent planet.[1]

Light Your Torch

Life is no brief candle to me.
It is sort of a splendid torch...
and I want to make it burn as brightly as possible
before handing it on to future generations.[2]

The smallest action is worth more than the greatest intention.

Everyone has a desire to at least come close to achieving their unique purpose in life. We have grand intentions but often fall short in converting intention to positive reality.

Although life's purpose varies from person to person, everyone shares at least one common purpose—to be a blessing to others. Accomplishing the common purpose requires us to be sensitive to issues blocking our progress and proactive in overcoming these obstacles. The nineteenth century psychologist and philosopher William James gave this sound advice: *Act as if what you do makes a difference. It does.*[3]

The Power of Action

More than 400 years ago, the Renaissance philosopher and author Sir Francis Bacon uttered this profound statement: "Knowledge is power."[4]

Though often quoted as fact, Sir Francis was not entirely correct. Knowledge is *potential* power. Until application is made, knowledge is nothing more than static matter. A more accurate observation and one worth remembering is: The *acquisition* of knowledge *plus* the *application* of knowledge is power! When acquired knowledge becomes applied knowledge, it moves from a *potential* state to an *active* state.

Albert Einstein published his theories of relativity in 1905 and again in 1916. His profound knowledge on the subject was made available in latent power form to the scientific community. Many years later, scientists acted on Einstein's ideas and research, i.e. his published knowledge, to develop the nuclear reactor and in 1945, to deliver the world's first atomic bomb. The *real* power in Einstein's knowledge came with the application of his ideas…and the world was forever changed!

The limitless reservoir of the human brain can store vast amounts of diverse knowledge for an entire lifetime—with room to spare! However, every byte of stockpiled knowledge lies dormant and of no practical value until actively applied.

The wise and prudent application of knowledge will produce sufficient personal power to revolutionize your life. It's not what you know that is important, it's what you *do* with what you know that matters!

The Power of Gratitude

Every person has an innate ability to recognize and appreciate the goodness and generosity of God and of friends, family, and business associates. We didn't ask for, purchase, or subscribe to this ability to feel gratefulness and express gratitude. They are loving gifts from our Creator.

Gratitude is a fundamental human value from which flows other positive attributes. When the force of gratitude is unrestricted within you, compassion, joy, contentment, and other expressions of gratefulness will saturate your life.

As we understand and acknowledge the enormity of blessings placed on us individually, as families, and as a free society, the power of gratitude flows unrestricted into our sphere of influence. Consider Melody Beattie's assessment of the phenomena:

> *Gratitude unlocks the fullness of life.*
> *It turns what we have into enough, and more.*
> *It turns denial into acceptance, chaos to order, confusion to clarity.*
> *It can turn a meal into a feast,*
> *a house into a home, a stranger into a friend.*[5]

Perhaps the most noteworthy attributes released by expressions of gratitude are kindness and generosity.

What is Kindness?

The famous British writer Aldous Huxley was a pioneer in the study of philosophies and techniques aimed at developing human potential. In a lecture given near the end of his life he said, "People

often ask me what is the most effective technique for transform-
ing their life. It is a little embarrassing that after years and years of
research and experimentation, I have to say that the best answer
is—just be a little kinder."[6]

Kindness is a language unto itself and transcends all boundar-
ies of ethnicity, socio-economic status, educational achievement,
and physical capabilities. The noted humorist and writer, Mark
Twain wisely described kindness thusly: *Kindness is a language
which the deaf can hear and the blind can read.*[7]

Kindness may be defined as an act that positively influences the
life of both the giver and the receiver. Genuine kindness typically
embodies some combination of humility, appreciation, respect,
and compassion. As you marinate your life daily with these quali-
ties and flavor it with a pinch of genuine thoughtfulness, you will
find yourself demonstrating frequent acts of kindness to friends,
associates, relatives, and even strangers.

Kindness is a little key that unlocks a huge treasure chest filled
with imperishable riches ready to decorate and transform your
life. Expressions of kindness polish the jewels of trust, appreciation, love, respect, and compassion. That's when joy and contentment begin to permeate your life and blend naturally into your
relationships.

Acts of kindness may be as extravagant as an expensive gift or
as simple as a few thoughtful words—written or spoken. Written
words, in particular, carry powerful and potentially enduring
messages. A handwritten (or at least personally signed) note or
letter will not be soon forgotten. Emails efficiently communicate
information, but handwritten notes convey feeling and emotion

and may be treasured as a statement directly from your heart to the recipient's heart.

Lord Byron, England's most famous nineteenth century poet captured the essence of word power in this phrase from *Don Juan:*

> *Words are things.*
> *And a small drop of ink,*
> *Falling like dew upon a thought*
> *Produces that which makes thousands,*
> *Perhaps millions, think.*[8]

Your words may convince a person that someone really *does* care. Your thoughtfulness may be the catalyst that rejuvenates their thinking and motivates them to proactively work toward a more meaningful, satisfying life. Indeed, your words may incite someone else to recognize the importance of expressing gratitude.

Whether the communication is verbal or written, your choice of words is critically important. Keep this timeless truth at the top of your mind in every situation: *People often forget what you say but rarely forget how you made them feel!*

Kindness satisfies an inborn need residing within the toughest scoundrel, the saintliest saint, and everyone in between. Everybody needs a little kindness, and the oftener it's received, the better it is! Remember, we're all more alike than we are different. *We are all angels with one wing, able to fly only when we embrace each other.*[9]

A Blind Man with Vision

In 1993, Chuck Wall was listening to the radio when a newscaster reported "yet another random act of senseless violence." As he thought about it, Wall wondered what would happen if he substituted 'kindness' for 'violence' in the equation.

As he pondered the implication of replacing the negative with a positive, Dr. Chuck Wall decided to test the proposition in the form of an assignment presented to his Human Relations and Communications class at Bakersfield College. He challenged his students with this assignment: "Go out and commit '*a random act of senseless kindness*' and write about your experience."

When the class met one week later, students ranging in age from twenty to fifty-five shared these amazing stories:

- Shane Gautreauz had distributed blankets bought from the Salvation Army to a group of homeless people living under Bakersfield's Beale Street overpass.

- Lisa Holiman rescued, bathed, and fed a ragged stray collie and put up posters to locate the dog's owners. One day later, the collie was reunited with its family.

- Jo Marshall, recently divorced after a thirty-seven-year marriage, set aside her anger and counseled her out-of-work former husband on how to extend his unemployment benefits.

- Perhaps the ultimate act of generosity for a student was committed by Jessica Fredericksen. Spying a harried motorist circling the student parking lot, Jessica backed out of the space she had just found and waved him into it.

Inspired by this unusual assignment, the students initiated a "kindness campaign" by printing and distributing bumper stickers containing this meaningful message: *Today, I will commit one random act of senseless kindness... Will you?*[20]

Today, Chuck Wall Ph.D. is Professor Emeritus at Bakersfield College and president of Kindness, Inc., a non-profit organization dedicated to encouraging kindness whenever and wherever it is needed.

Even though Dr. Wall is blind, he does not consider himself disabled. He says he merely must spend extra time dealing with one of life's little nuisances.[11]

Kindness is Basic Equipment

We are designed to be kind. When the Creator chose to make us in his own image, he included a vast reservoir of potential good deeds patiently waiting to be activated. He gently nudges us in the right direction as we study the writings of the Apostle Paul:

> And be ye kind one to another,
> tenderhearted, forgiving one another,
> even as God, for Christ's sake, hath forgiven you.
>
> —Ephesians 4:32 (KJV)

Pay particular attention to the word *tenderhearted* in this instruction from God. Literally, it means that we are to treat others with gentleness, tenderness, sensitivity, compassion, and when appropriate, sympathy.

Sometimes, we to try to bend God's rules and end up breaking them. We become, in a sense, a prodigal child—bent on having our own way. When you are in a "prodigal" mood, remember that

1. You personally have been richly blessed.
2. Every good gift and rich blessing is from God.

The Prodigal

When I'm a prodigal, lean grocer's shelves aggravate me,
But when I'm in sync with my Father's will,
I remember the millions hungering for just one slice of bread,
While I could buy hundreds of *loaves* today.
Ah, God, You're so good to me!

When I'm a prodigal, children's incessant questions irritate me,
But when I'm in sync with my Father's will,
I remember children are created with an expansive, empty database
And they ask *me* questions out of respect for my wisdom.
Ah, God, You're so good to me!

When I'm a prodigal, people—even friends—can be so annoying!
But when I'm in sync with my Father's will,
I remember that He places people in my path for a purpose; so
I may be a blessing to them…or they may be a blessing to me!
Ah, God, You're so good to me!

When I'm a prodigal, I see our flag as just a colored rag.
But when I'm in sync with my Father's will,
The stars and stripes remind me of scores of children who will
never come home again;
Those who died so I can breathe the fresh air of freedom.
Ah, God, You're so good to me!

When I'm a prodigal, I'm so self-centered...life is all about me!
But when I'm in sync with my Father's will,
I realize that I'm a small—but *important*—part of His plan,
And walking close to Him, my life will be an incredible journey.
Ah, God, You're so *very* good to me!

—J. Carl Newell

What is Kindness Worth?

What is the value of a glass of water?

If you're watching the Super Bowl on a widescreen HDTV with a well-stocked refrigerator just fifty feet from your recliner, you're not interested in purchasing a glass of water.

But if your 4WD SUV blew a gasket thirty-five miles from the nearest road in the southwest Arizona desert, water would have an astronomical value. Wandering lost and alone over this vast cactus and rattlesnake-infested wilderness with swollen tongue and parched lips, your unheard cry would be, "*I would give everything I have in this world for one glass of water!*"

The essential value of kindness is obviously incalculable but like quality, we know it when we see it. Authentic value is determined by the level of need in the lives of the persons involved. Every person is unique and therefore has—to some degree—a unique value system. However, everyone seems to long for and appreciate the *little* things in life.

A gentle touch, a kind word, a smile, an honest compliment, a listening ear, or some unexpected act of kindness to the right person, in the right way, at the right time is of immeasurable value.

The Generosity Factor

Another important facet of gratitude is generosity. As a society, we generously support charitable organizations. When national and international crises develop, Americans notably respond by supporting recovery efforts through prayer and contributions of money, supplies, time, and expertise.

One of the wonders of life is that *when we give, we receive.* Realizing this phenomenon, the American philosopher and essayist Ralph Waldo Emerson made this observation: *It is one of the most beautiful compensations of life that no man can sincerely try to help another without helping himself.*[12]

Emerson was echoing a portion of Jesus' teaching recorded more than 1800 years earlier by Dr. Luke:

> Give, and it will be given to you.
> A good measure, pressed down, shaken together
> and running over, will be poured into your lap.

> Luke 6:38a

The crux of Jesus' lesson reaches much deeper than money and material assets. This is an all-encompassing "give"...a continual giving action whereby you give your time and energy, respect and consideration, understanding and acceptance of others—in spite of their status—and most importantly, you give *yourself* to help satisfy the needs of others.

When you make unselfish, unrestrained giving a habit, you will see incredible results. Amazingly, you may never even know the ultimate effects of your generosity; it will touch lives well beyond your circle of friends and acquaintances.

Keep Your Light Shining

"This little light of mine, I'm gonna let it shine!"

Remember singing those words when you were a child? You probably sang with joy in your heart and a big smile on your face. Why? Because deep within your being, you sensed a relationship between your attitude and accomplishing God's purpose in your life.

As you face each day with an optimistic, enthusiastic attitude, you will see more and more opportunities to positively affect the lives of people who need a "lift." Develop the habit of looking for opportunities to brighten someone else's day.

Every person has been given a specific assignment by God. Some are called to influence millions while others are expected to influence a relative few. The inescapable fact however, is that *everybody's* life assignment includes the responsibility to proactively be sensitive to the needs of others.

Sharing the spark of our light with others can begin reversing the global cooling effects within our own small world and enable others to do likewise.

The spark from one fire lights another fire, and
there is a wind that blows down the path of history.
The spark that we send down the wind
will ignite later generations.
It will not die.[13]

The Bridge Builder

An old man, going a lone highway,
Came at the evening, cold and gray,
To a chasm, vast and deep and wide,
Through which was flowing a sullen tide.

The old man crossed in the twilight dim,
The sullen stream had no fears for him,
But he turned when safe on the other side
And built a bridge to span the tide.

"Old man," said a fellow pilgrim near,
"You are wasting strength with building here,
Your journey will end with the ending day,
You never again must pass this way,
You have crossed the chasm, deep and wide—
Why build you the bridge at the eventide?"

The builder lifted his old gray head:
"Good friend, in the path I have come," he said,
"There followeth after me today
A youth whose feet must pass this way.

This chasm that has been naught to me
To that fair-haired youth may a pitfall be,
He, too must cross in the twilight dim;
Good friend, I am building the bridge for him."

—Will Allen Dromgoole[14]

Ninety-nine percent of everything you do in life is attitude. If you have a relationship with God and you have the right attitude, you're going to ask the one question in life that covers everything: "How can I help you?"[1]

The Gratitude Attitude

An attitude of gratitude should flavor everything you do.[2]

Life is complex in its simplicity.

At birth, the Creator blessed you with a wonderfully simple, yet amazingly powerful, gift. As you understand the power of this gift and make wise application on a daily basis, your ability to design and live a prosperous and contented life will become reality.

Your gift is the greatest power anyone can possess...the power of personal choice.

The power of choice is a priceless possession. It is the highway that can take you anywhere in life you want to go. You must decide where you want to go and maintain a strong enough desire to work in that direction.

Your greatest power is the power to choose!

Your Attitude: A Powerful Choice

Every morning when your feet hit the floor, you decide—either consciously or subconsciously—your attitude for the day. Most of us exhibit the same attitude day after day because as with breathing, our attitude has become an unconscious habit.

Mr. Webster's first definition of attitude is commonly understood and accepted. Initially, however, his second description of the word seems to have little or no applicability to our personal life.

> **at·ti·tude** [áttə tud], noun
> **1a** : a manner of acting, feeling or thinking that shows one's disposition, opinion, etc. **b** : a mental position with regard to a fact or state.
>
> **2** : In *aeronautics*, the position of an aircraft or spacecraft determined by the relationship between its axes and a reference datum (as the horizon or a particular star).

Cruising at an altitude of nearly 60,000 feet and airspeed of 1,336 miles per hour—twice the speed of sound—British Airways' Concorde was the fastest commercial passenger aircraft in the world. A ground speed of 215 knots (approximately 247 mph) is required for Concorde to take off.

Imagine the Concorde roaring down the runway without the pilot ever pulling back on the yoke to change the aircraft's *attitude*, permitting it to become airborne. The resulting crash would be life-changing devastation to the hundreds of people onboard and potentially thousands of family members, friends, and associates.

Now, imagine your life as a supersonic aircraft fully loaded with precious cargo…your family and loved-ones, friends, and all your dreams for the future. You are the pilot—the only person with the ability to realign your attitude.

This analogy may be personalized and made relevant to yourself by considering the effects your attitude has on what happens in your life. We often allow self-serving attitudes to propel our "aircraft" down life's runway at a flat-out speed without much regard to the enormous effect our actions have on ourselves, our future, and the precious cargo entrusted to us.

Ask yourself, "Is my attitude usually conducive to nurturing and developing the quality of life I desire for myself and those I love?" Unless the answer is an unqualified, "Yes!" you should reevaluate your position and consider developing new attitudes.

Why Should I?

That's a good question considering the widespread perception that since we're all in this life together, common threads of happenstance unite us. For example, the rain continues to fall on the just and the unjust, good things still happen to bad people and bad things still happen to good people. Therefore, this logic surmises, we're all cool...we're okay!

This reasoning contains at least two critical flaws:

1. The Creator expects *you* to fully accept responsibility for your life.

2. God's richest blessings are poured out on those who strive to meet His expectations.

God's desire is to provide everything we need to become the very best person possible. The choice is ours to accept or decline His blessings.

> "For I know the plans I have for you," declares the Lord,
> "plans to prosper you and not to harm you,
> plans to give you hope and a future."
>
> Jeremiah 29:11

The 100% Rule

I am responsible for my life and well-being;
For my thoughts and the visions I see.
Life is not always lovely—I'll agree;
Nevertheless, I am 100% responsible for me.

I am responsible for my attitude, my behavior
And the circumstances they cause to be.
I can laugh or cry, be shy or act boldly,
For I am 100% responsible for me.

I am responsible for all my decisions
And daily blessed with opportunities.
I can make my life a terrific place to be,
For I am totally, 100% responsible for me!

—J. Carl Newell

Where's the Problem?

More than 110 years ago, the United States Supreme Court declared the United States a Christian nation.[3] Poll results released in March 2002 indicated that 67% of Americans believe that the United States is a Christian nation.[4] More recently, when pollsters asked Americans to "categorize your faith," 85% claimed to be a Christian.[5]

So, where's the problem? Why are so many professing Christians living—as Thoreau observed—lives of quiet desperation?

Harry Blamires[6], in his critically acclaimed book *The Christian Mind,* has said that while Christians may worship and pray as Christians, they do not *think* as Christians. Until you have some understanding of what God requires of you and begin to *think* like a Christian, expect your life to remain shallow and unsatisfying.

Nearly 3000 years ago, the prophet Micah recorded God's bottom-line expectations for humankind:

> He has showed you, O man, what is good. And what does the Lord require of you? To act justly and to love mercy and to walk humbly with your God.
>
> Micah 6:8

Think about It!

An aphorism is a wise saying that bears repeating. The ancient Greek philosopher Socrates gave some very wise counsel as he spoke this profound aphorism: *The unexamined life is not worth living.*

Tens of thousands of books have been written to give insight on "how to" be a better person and have an awesome life. But without question, the Bible is the absolute best, most effective self-help book ever written. As you examine your life in the light of God's Word, you will find clarity and begin to make meaningful progress on your life's adventure.

What solution does the Bible offer to the problem defined by Harry Blamires as "Christians...do not *think* as Christians"? Acknowledging that you are 100% responsible for your own life, consider this lesson from God's Word: "Do not conform any longer to the pattern of this world, but be transformed by the renewing of your mind" (Romans 12:2).

The lesson is clear: You can follow the crowd down the road of discouragement, depression, and defeat *or* you can *choose* to "think as a Christian," renew your mind, and transform your life. *The choice is yours!*

Another biblical lesson is in the form of a directive: "Let this mind be in you, which was also in Christ Jesus" (Philippians 2:5 KJV).

Again, the lesson is crystal clear. The word *let* suggests that an option—or a choice—is available to you. You can continue nurturing the old patterns of thinking, which brought you to where you are in life, *or* you can *choose* to "think as a Christian" by seeking to have the "mind of Christ." *The choice is yours!*

Obviously, none of us can attain the pure perfection of Christ's mind, but we can choose to practice the attributes exemplified by his humility, love, and gratitude as he walked the earth as a physical being.

Choose an attitude of gratitude!

An Attitude of Gratitude

Living our routine, everyday life, many of us who should know better, struggle with accepting these realities:

1. Life is not about *me.*
2. Life is not about *you.*
3. Life is about *us!*

Since the quality of your life depends on the quality of your relationships, it's a good idea to develop the habit of being "others oriented."

An attitude of gratitude generates a desire to perform acts of kindness that enable you to daily fulfill God's requirement to "love mercy." The people whose lives are touched will be blessed, and you will experience the blessings of satisfaction, joy, and contentment that always accompany obedience to God.

There is no better time than right now to choose—and live—a life governed by an attitude of gratitude. *Start today!*

Today

Today is mine. It is unique.

Nobody else in the world has a today exactly like mine.

Today contains the sum of all my past experience
and all my future potential.

Today will become what I choose to make it!

I can choose to fill today with joyful moments.

Or I can choose to saturate today
with anxious and worrisome thoughts.

It is my choice…for today is mine!

—J. Carl Newell

Lord, teach me to appreciate what I have
before time forces me to appreciate what I had.

The Gratitude Journal

The palest ink is better than the best memory.

—Chinese proverb

Our best intentions and grand ideas are often lost forever!

Have you ever had a flash of inspiration in the morning and by late afternoon, could remember only that there was something you didn't want to forget? It happens to us all!

There's no real difficulty in originating good ideas or formulating a plan to repay a compliment, send a thank-you note, or make an encouraging telephone call to a friend. The difficulty is in retrieving the necessary information from its storage space in your brain…and doing it!

When you are constantly caught up in a vortex of schedules, games, agendas, going, doing, meeting, planning, worrying, deadlines, and rushing from here to there, it's easy to neglect things you *really* want to do. Excessive busyness sucks the joy out of life and leaves you physically and emotionally drained.

Life really is full of joy and beauty…if you take the time to seek it. Our hectic twenty-first century life is not nearly as oppressive as the two years endured by a thirteen-year-old Jewish girl hiding in a secret room to avoid the Nazi holocaust. Within those dreadful circumstances, Anne Frank wrote this note in her diary: *Think of all the beauty still left around you and be happy.*[1]

When you develop the habit of stepping aside from life's pressures for a few minutes each day, you can catch your breath, relax, and enjoy the blessings you've received. This *Gratitude Journal* has been created to help you develop the habit of living a more satisfying and better quality life.

Rejuvenate Your Life!

Life is full of beginnings...every hour, every day.

Most are very small beginnings: One raindrop is the beginning of a flood; one acorn is the beginning of a mighty oak tree. Forest fires are ignited from one spark; one small idea can revolutionize the world.

Your quest for a more satisfying life can begin with this one small assertion: I *choose* to express gratitude for blessings received and to be a blessing to someone else as often as possible. Once this affirmation is internalized and practiced for twenty-one days, it will become a worthwhile habit that will enhance your life.

The *Gratitude Journal* consists of fifty-two sets of pages, one set per week for one year. Each weekly set is divided into five sections: My Gratitude Journal, My IOTAs, a Bible verse, Nuggets of Wisdom and a personal Pass It On List.

My Gratitude Journal

The exercise of writing ideas, reflections about people, and events and blessings you've received is an invaluable experience. This process keeps life in perspective and enables you to capitalize on the full value of your life experiences.

Think of this small journal as a *storage container* for ideas, thoughts, self-reflection, deeds to be done, and initial plans for future self-development activities.

Make it a goal to keep your journal entries positive. Research has shown that in general, optimistic, grateful, and loving thoughts result in the release of "feel good" neurotransmitters called endorphins in the brain.

Learning to focus on the positive can do wonders for your energy level, as well as improve health and longevity. Other research suggests that when people train themselves to feel love and gratitude regularly, their blood pressure normalizes, their heart function stabilizes, and they have more energy.[2]

For maximum benefit, journal entries should be reviewed at least twice daily: early each morning and immediately before turning out the light at bedtime. Concentrating on your journal at bedtime saturates your subconscious mind with positive thoughts of blessing and gratefulness as you drift into sleep.

My IOTAs

IOTA is a mnemonic for *Ideas, Observations, Thoughts,* and *Affirmations.* This free-form area can replace those notes written on scraps of paper and the backs of business cards that are soon misplaced or forgotten.

IOTAs are a permanent record of information you want to keep readily available for future consideration or action.

Bible Verses

The Bible is the most effective road map available for living a gratifying life. However, unless you *choose* to review and remember God's Word, it will be unavailable when time and circumstances create a longing within you for its comforting message.

Each section includes wisdom from God's Word that will be extremely beneficial to your mental and spiritual health as you contemplate each week's message.

You may ask, "Why should I consider memorizing scripture?" Here are several excellent reasons for developing this discipline:

1. *It is therapeutic...it's good for your mental health.*

    ⊰ *A man is what he thinks about all day long.*

    —Ralph Waldo Emerson

    ⊰ *Change your thoughts and you change your world.*

    —Norman Vincent Peale

For as he thinketh in his heart, so is he.

—Proverbs 23:7a (KJV)

Charles L. Allen, a prominent Methodist minister and pastor, authored many books, including *God's Psychiatry*, *Perfect Peace*, and *The Twenty-third Psalm (An Interpretation)*. Dr. Allen often wrote this "prescription" for those whom he counseled:

> *Read the 23rd Psalm five times daily for seven days.*
> *Read it thoughtfully and unhurriedly first thing upon*
> *getting-up in the morning, immediately after breakfast,*
> *after lunch, after dinner and just before going to bed.*[3]

Dr. Allen reported amazing results in the lives of people who followed this advice for meditating on God's Word.

2. *God's speaks to us through His Word.* The power is not in memorizing the words, but rather in thinking the thoughts and having your mind tuned in to God.

3. *God's Word brings us comfort and assurance.* Near the end of his life, the eminent scientist Michael Faraday was visited by a friend who tried to introduce some levity into the situation. The well-wisher said, "Sir Michael, what speculations have you now?"

Taking the question seriously, Faraday replied, "Speculations, man, I have none. I have certainties. I thank God that I don't rest my dying head upon speculations for *"I know whom I have believed, and am persuaded that He is able to keep that which I have committed unto Him against that day.*"[4] Notice that Faraday was comforted by scripture he had memorized (2 Timothy 1:12).

Nuggets of Wisdom

Not unlike memorizing scripture, meditating on wise sayings and timeless truths makes valuable deposits into your memory bank.

Whether in a business setting or communicating with friends, flavoring your message with fascinating illustrations or memorable quotes makes a positive impact. Johann Wolfgang von Goethe— the eighteenth century German philosopher, dramatist, poet and scientist, summed up the point this way:

> *All truly wise thoughts have been thought already*
> *thousands of times; but to make them truly ours,*
> *we must think them over again honestly,*
> *until they take root in our personal experience.*

Pass It On List

The drama/romance film *Pay It Forward*[5] was based on the idea of doing good deeds. The storyline has a seventh grade teacher giving his students a class project to "think of a way to change our world and put it into action."

A student named Trevor lives with his alcoholic mother who works in a seedy Las Vegas bar. Trevor's idea to "change the world" is to take three actions that make a difference in the lives of others and ask each of those people to do likewise for three other people and so on, ad infinitum.

While the Pass It On List has no such mind-expanding goal, it simply encourages you to jot down good deeds you wish to perform, review them often, and check them off when completed.

You may want to record the date and some commentary to remind you of the event in the future.

Now…it's time to begin your Gratitude Journal!

1

My Gratitude Journal

People, events, and activities for which I am thoughtfully and specifically grateful this week:

1. _____

2. _____

3. _____

4. _____

5. _____

My IOTAs

Ideas, Observations, Thoughts, and *Affirmations* I want to record and remember for future consideration:

_____

_____

_____

_____

_____

Give thanks in all circumstances,
for this is God's will for you in Christ Jesus.

—1 Thessalonians 5:18

When you don't get everything you want,
be thankful for the things
you don't get
that you don't want!

Pass It On List

❑ _____

❑ _____

❑ _____

❑ _____

❑ _____

2

My Gratitude Journal

People, events, and activities for which I am thoughtfully and specifically grateful this week:

1. _____

2. _____

3. _____

4. _____

5. _____

My IOTAs

Ideas, Observations, Thoughts, and *Affirmations* I want to record and remember for future consideration:

_____

_____

_____

_____

_____

Do not let any unwholesome talk
come out of your mouths, but only
what is helpful for building others up
according to their needs,
that it may benefit those who listen.

—Ephesians 4:29

There is a time to speak
and a time to keep quiet.
There are things to tell
and things not to tell.

—B. C. Forbes (1880–1954)
Scottish journalist, Founder of *Forbes Magazine*

Pass It On List

❏ _____

❏ _____

❏ _____

❏ _____

❏ _____

3
My Gratitude Journal

People, events, and activities for which I am thoughtfully and specifically grateful this week:

1. _____

2. _____

3. _____

4. _____

5. _____

My IOTAs

Ideas, Observations, Thoughts, and *Affirmations* I want to record and remember for future consideration:

_____

_____

_____

_____

_____

Show me your ways, O Lord,
teach me your paths;
guide me in your truth and teach me,
for you are God my Savior,
and my hope is in you all day long.

—Psalm 25:4–5

Lord, teach me to appreciate
what I have
before time forces me to appreciate
what I had.

Pass It On List

❏ _____

❏ _____

❏ _____

❏ _____

❏ _____

4
My Gratitude Journal

People, events, and activities for which I am thoughtfully and specifically grateful this week:

1. _____

2. _____

3. _____

4. _____

5. _____

My IOTAs

Ideas, Observations, Thoughts, and *Affirmations* I want to record and remember for future consideration:

_____

_____

_____

_____

_____

A generous man will prosper;
he who refreshes others
will himself be refreshed.

—Proverbs 11:25

A hundred times a day,
I remind myself that my inner and outer life
depends on the labors of other men,
living and dead,
and that I must exert myself
in order to give in the same measure
as I have received.

Albert Einstein (1879 - 1955)
German-born Jewish theoretical physicist

Pass It On List

❏ _____

❏ _____

❏ _____

❏ _____

❏ _____

5
My Gratitude Journal

People, events, and activities for which I am thoughtfully and specifically grateful this week:

1. _____

2. _____

3. _____

4. _____

5. _____

My IOTAs

Ideas, Observations, Thoughts, and *Affirmations* I want to record and remember for future consideration:

_____

_____

_____

_____

_____

Sow your seed in the morning,
and at evening let not your hands be idle,
for you do not know which will succeed,
whether this or that,
or whether both will do equally well.

—Ecclesiastes 11:6

Resolve to perform what you ought;
perform without fail what you resolve.

—Benjamin Franklin (1706–1790)
American statesman, writer and scientist

Pass It On List

❑ _____

❑ _____

❑ _____

❑ _____

❑ _____

6
My Gratitude Journal

People, events, and activities for which I am thoughtfully and specifically grateful this week:

1. _____

2. _____

3. _____

4. _____

5. _____

My IOTAs

Ideas, Observations, Thoughts, and *Affirmations* I want to record and remember for future consideration:

_____

_____

_____

_____

_____

Can two walk together except they be agreed?

—Amos 3:3 (KJV)

I can do what you can't do
and you can do what I can't do.
Together, we can do great things!

—Mother Teresa (1910–1997)
Missionary to the poor in Calcutta, India

Pass It On List

❏ _____

❏ _____

❏ _____

❏ _____

❏ _____

7
My Gratitude Journal

People, events, and activities for which I am thoughtfully and specifically grateful this week:

1. _____

2. _____

3. _____

4. _____

5. _____

My IOTAs

Ideas, Observations, Thoughts, and *Affirmations* I want to record and remember for future consideration:

_____

_____

_____

_____

_____

Do not be anxious about anything,
but in everything, by prayer and petition,
with thanksgiving, present your requests to God.
And the peace of God,
which transcends all understanding,
will guard your hearts and your minds
in Christ Jesus.

—Philippians 4:6–7

The happiness of your life depends on
the quality of your thoughts.

—Marcus Aurelius (121–180)
Roman Emperor

Pass It On List

❑ _____

❑ _____

❑ _____

❑ _____

❑ _____

8
My Gratitude Journal

People, events, and activities for which I am thoughtfully and specifically grateful this week:

1. _____

2. _____

3. _____

4. _____

5. _____

My IOTAs

Ideas, Observations, Thoughts, and *Affirmations* I want to record and remember for future consideration:

_____

_____

_____

_____

_____

Let your eyes look straight ahead,
fix your gaze directly before you.
Make level paths for your feet and
take only ways that are firm.

—Proverbs 4:25–26

The quality of a man's life is in direct proportion
to his commitment to excellence.

—Vince Lombardi (1913–1970)
Legendary NFL Coach

Pass It On List

❑ _____

❑ _____

❑ _____

❑ _____

❑ _____

9
My Gratitude Journal

People, events, and activities for which I am thoughtfully and specifically grateful this week:

1. _____

2. _____

3. _____

4. _____

5. _____

My IOTAs

Ideas, Observations, Thoughts, and *Affirmations* I want to record and remember for future consideration:

_____

_____

_____

_____

_____

If any of you lacks wisdom,
he should ask God,
who gives generously to all
without finding fault,
and it will be given to him.

—James 1:5

He is a wise man who does not grieve
for the things which he has not,
but rejoices for those which he has.

—Epictetus (55–135)
Greek philosopher

Pass It On List

❏ _____

❏ _____

❏ _____

❏ _____

❏ _____

10
My Gratitude Journal

People, events, and activities for which I am thoughtfully and specifically grateful this week:

1. _____

2. _____

3. _____

4. _____

5. _____

My IOTAs

Ideas, Observations, Thoughts, and *Affirmations* I want to record and remember for future consideration:

_____

_____

_____

_____

_____

For we are God's workmanship,
created in Christ Jesus to do good works,
which God prepared in advance for us to do.

—Ephesians 2:10

My life is a gift to me from my Creator.
What I do with my life is my gift back to my Creator.
—Billy Mills
Olympic Gold Medal Winner - 1964

Pass It On List

❑ _____

❑ _____

❑ _____

❑ _____

❑ _____

11

My Gratitude Journal

People, events, and activities for which I am thoughtfully and specifically grateful this week:

1. _____

2. _____

3. _____

4. _____

5. _____

My IOTAs

Ideas, Observations, Thoughts, and *Affirmations* I want to record and remember for future consideration:

_____

_____

_____

_____

_____

But remember the Lord your God,
for it is he who gives you
the ability to produce wealth.

—Deuteronomy 8:18a

Everything I am or ever shall be and
everything I have or ever shall have,
are manifestations of God's grace in my life.

Pass It On List

❑ _____

❑ _____

❑ _____

❑ _____

❑ _____

12
My Gratitude Journal

People, events, and activities for which I am thoughtfully and specifically grateful this week:

1. _____

2. _____

3. _____

4. _____

5. _____

My IOTAs

Ideas, Observations, Thoughts, and *Affirmations* I want to record and remember for future consideration:

_____

_____

_____

_____

_____

A word aptly spoken
is like apples of gold
in settings of silver.

—Proverbs 25:11

Feeling gratitude and not expressing it
is like wrapping a present
and not giving it.

—William Arthur Ward (1921–1997)
American minister and author

Pass It On List

❏ _____

❏ _____

❏ _____

❏ _____

❏ _____

13
My Gratitude Journal

People, events, and activities for which I am thoughtfully and specifically grateful this week:

1. _____

2. _____

3. _____

4. _____

5. _____

My IOTAs

Ideas, Observations, Thoughts, and *Affirmations* I want to record and remember for future consideration:

_____

_____

_____

_____

_____

Do to others
as you would have them
do to you.

—Luke 6:31

It is one of the most beautiful
compensations of life that no man
can sincerely try to help another
without helping himself.

—Ralph Waldo Emerson (1803–1882)
American essayist and philosopher

Pass It On List

❑ _____

❑ _____

❑ _____

❑ _____

❑ _____

14
My Gratitude Journal

People, events, and activities for which I am thoughtfully and specifically grateful this week:

1. _____

2. _____

3. _____

4. _____

5. _____

My IOTAs

Ideas, Observations, Thoughts, and *Affirmations* I want to record and remember for future consideration:

_____

_____

_____

_____

_____

Do not boast about tomorrow,
for you do not know what a day may bring forth.

—Proverbs 27:2

Yesterday is history.
Tomorrow is a mystery.
Today is a gift,
That's why it's called the present.

Pass It On List

❑ _____

❑ _____

❑ _____

❑ _____

❑ _____

15
My Gratitude Journal

People, events, and activities for which I am thoughtfully and specifically grateful this week:

1. _____

2. _____

3. _____

4. _____

5. _____

My IOTAs

Ideas, Observations, Thoughts, and *Affirmations* I want to record and remember for future consideration:

_____

_____

_____

_____

_____

If the Lord delights in a man's way,
he makes his steps firm;
though he stumble, he will not fall
for the Lord upholds him with his hand.

—Psalm 37:23–24

Never confuse a single defeat with a final defeat.
—F. Scott Fitzgerald (1896–1940)
American novelist

Pass It On List

❏ _____

❏ _____

❏ _____

❏ _____

❏ _____

16
My Gratitude Journal

People, events, and activities for which I am thoughtfully and specifically grateful this week:

1. _____

2. _____

3. _____

4. _____

5. _____

My IOTAs

Ideas, Observations, Thoughts, and *Affirmations* I want to record and remember for future consideration:

_____

_____

_____

_____

_____

I can do all things through Christ,
who strengtheneth me.

—Philippians 4:13 (KJV)

Where the willingness is great,
the difficulties cannot be great.

—Niccolo Machiavelli (1469–1527)
Italian statesman and philosopher

Pass It On List

❑ _____

❑ _____

❑ _____

❑ _____

❑ _____

17
My Gratitude Journal

People, events, and activities for which I am thoughtfully and specifically grateful this week:

1. _____

2. _____

3. _____

4. _____

5. _____

My IOTAs

Ideas, Observations, Thoughts, and *Affirmations* I want to record and remember for future consideration:

_____

_____

_____

_____

_____

Trust in the Lord with all your heart
and lean not on your own understanding;
in all your ways acknowledge him,
and he will make your paths straight.

—Proverbs 3:5–6

If you continue to do what's right,
what's wrong and who's wrong
will eventually leave your life.

—David Blunt
Pastor, Church on the Rock
St. Peters, MO

Pass It On List

❑ _____

❑ _____

❑ _____

❑ _____

❑ _____

18
My Gratitude Journal

People, events, and activities for which I am thoughtfully and specifically grateful this week:

1. _____

2. _____

3. _____

4. _____

5. _____

My IOTAs

Ideas, Observations, Thoughts, and *Affirmations* I want to record and remember for future consideration:

_____

_____

_____

_____

_____

He has shown thee, O man, what is good;
and what doth the Lord require of thee, but
and to do justly and to love mercy
to walk humbly with thy God?

—Micah 6:9 (KJV)

Make it a habit to transmute time
into service, wealth, or wisdom.
Be a good steward of all your moments!

Pass It On List

☐ _____

☐ _____

☐ _____

☐ _____

☐ _____

19
My Gratitude Journal

People, events, and activities for which I am thoughtfully and specifically grateful this week:

1. _____

2. _____

3. _____

4. _____

5. _____

My IOTAs

Ideas, Observations, Thoughts, and *Affirmations* I want to record and remember for future consideration:

_____

_____

_____

_____

_____

I have hidden your word in my heart
that I might not sin against you.

—Psalm 119:11

A thorough knowledge of the Bible
is worth more than a college education.

—Theodore Roosevelt (1858–1919)
26th President of the United States

Pass It On List

❏ _____

❏ _____

❏ _____

❏ _____

❏ _____

20
My Gratitude Journal

People, events, and activities for which I am thoughtfully and specifically grateful this week:

1. _____

2. _____

3. _____

4. _____

5. _____

My IOTAs

Ideas, Observations, Thoughts, and *Affirmations* I want to record and remember for future consideration:

_____

_____

_____

_____

_____

And you will know the truth and
the truth will set you free.

—John 8:32

The truth is incontrovertible.
Malaise may attack it and
ignorance may divide it, but
in the end, there it is.

—Sir Winston Churchill (1874–1965)
British Prime Minister

Pass It On List

❑ _____

❑ _____

❑ _____

❑ _____

❑ _____

21
My Gratitude Journal

People, events, and activities for which I am thoughtfully and specifically grateful this week:

1. _____

2. _____

3. _____

4. _____

5. _____

My IOTAs

Ideas, Observations, Thoughts, and *Affirmations* I want to record and remember for future consideration:

_____

_____

_____

_____

_____

He who pursues righteousness and love
finds life, prosperity and honor.

—Psalm 21:21

It's a funny thing about life:
If you refuse to accept anything but the best,
you very often get it.

W. Somerset Maugham (1874–1965)
British author

Pass It On List

❑ _____

❑ _____

❑ _____

❑ _____

❑ _____

22
My Gratitude Journal

People, events, and activities for which I am thoughtfully and specifically grateful this week:

1. _____

2. _____

3. _____

4. _____

5. _____

My IOTAs

Ideas, Observations, Thoughts, and *Affirmations* I want to record and remember for future consideration:

_____

_____

_____

_____

_____

Commit your way to the Lord;
trust in him and he will do this:
He will make your righteousness
shine like the dawn,
the justice of your cause
like the noonday sun.

—Psalm 37:5–6

Jesus is the only person
who can control your life
without destroying it.

Pass It On List

❑ _____

❑ _____

❑ _____

❑ _____

❑ _____

23
My Gratitude Journal

People, events, and activities for which I am thoughtfully and specifically grateful this week:

1. _____

2. _____

3. _____

4. _____

5. _____

My IOTAs

Ideas, Observations, Thoughts, and *Affirmations* I want to record and remember for future consideration:

_____

_____

_____

_____

_____

Even a fool is thought wise
if he keeps silent,
and discerning if he holds his tongue.

—Proverbs 17:28

Remember to not only say the right thing
at the right time in the right place,
but far more difficult still,
to leave unsaid the wrong thing
at the wrong moment.

—Benjamin Franklin (1706–1790)
American statesman, writer and scientist

Pass It On List

❑ _____

❑ _____

❑ _____

❑ _____

❑ _____

24
My Gratitude Journal

People, events, and activities for which I am thoughtfully and specifically grateful this week:

1. _____

2. _____

3. _____

4. _____

5. _____

My IOTAs

Ideas, Observations, Thoughts, and *Affirmations* I want to record and remember for future consideration:

_____

_____

_____

_____

_____

Do not conform any longer
to the pattern of this world,
but be transformed
by the renewing of your mind.

—Romans 12:2a

The greatest discovery of my generation
is that man can alter his life
simply by altering his attitude of mind.

—William James (1842–1910)
American psychologist and philosopher

Pass It On List

❑ _____

❑ _____

❑ _____

❑ _____

❑ _____

25

My Gratitude Journal

People, events, and activities for which I am thoughtfully and specifically grateful this week:

1. _____

2. _____

3. _____

4. _____

5. _____

My IOTAs

Ideas, Observations, Thoughts, and *Affirmations* I want to record and remember for future consideration:

_____

_____

_____

_____

_____

For God hath not given us the spirit of fear
but of power and of love
and of a sound mind.

—2 Timothy 1:7 (KJV)

It is better to be a lion for a day
than a sheep all your life.

—Sister Elizabeth Kenny (1880–1952)
Australian nurse; a pioneer in treatment for polio

Pass It On List

❑ _____

❑ _____

❑ _____

❑ _____

❑ _____

26
My Gratitude Journal

People, events, and activities for which I am thoughtfully and specifically grateful this week:

1. _____

2. _____

3. _____

4. _____

5. _____

My IOTAs

Ideas, Observations, Thoughts, and *Affirmations* I want to record and remember for future consideration:

_____

_____

_____

_____

_____

Have I not commanded you?
Be strong and courageous.
Do not be terrified; do not be discouraged,
for the Lord your God
will be with you wherever you go.

—Joshua 1:9

Courage is not the absence of fear,
but rather the judgment that
something else is more important than fear.

—Ambrose Redmoon (1930–1996)
American writer

Pass It On List

❏ _____

❏ _____

❏ _____

❏ _____

❏ _____

27
My Gratitude Journal

People, events, and activities for which I am thoughtfully and specifically grateful this week:

1. _____

2. _____

3. _____

4. _____

5. _____

My IOTAs

Ideas, Observations, Thoughts, and *Affirmations* I want to record and remember for future consideration:

_____

_____

_____

_____

_____

I know the plans I have for you, declares the Lord,
plans to prosper you and not to harm you,
plans to give you hope and a future.

—Jeremiah 29:11

Cherish your vision and your dreams,
as they are the children of your soul,
the blueprints of your ultimate achievements.

—Napoleon Hill (1883–1970)
American author

Pass It On List

❏ _____

❏ _____

❏ _____

❏ _____

❏ _____

28
My Gratitude Journal

People, events, and activities for which I am thoughtfully and specifically grateful this week:

1. _____

2. _____

3. _____

4. _____

5. _____

My IOTAs

Ideas, Observations, Thoughts, and *Affirmations* I want to record and remember for future consideration:

_____

_____

_____

_____

_____

The Broom

God knocked on the door of my heart one day
And I looked for a place to hide.

My soul was cluttered and choked with debris
And things were untidy inside.

There were tasks neglected, long overdue;
Cobwebs to be brushed from the wall.

Rugs to be shaken and windows cleaned up...
I had not expected His call!

I stood with my hand on the latch of the door
And gazed at the mess in the room.

When I opened the door, my soul blushed to see,
God had left on my doorstep, a broom!

—Author Unknown

Pass It On List

❑ _____

❑ _____

❑ _____

❑ _____

❑ _____

29
My Gratitude Journal

People, events, and activities for which I am thoughtfully and specifically grateful this week:

1. _____

2. _____

3. _____

4. _____

5. _____

My IOTAs

Ideas, Observations, Thoughts, and *Affirmations* I want to record and remember for future consideration:

_____

_____

_____

_____

_____

The fear of the Lord
is the beginning of knowledge,
but fools despise wisdom and discipline.

—Proverbs 1:7

On the bookshelf of life,
God is a useful work of reference,
always at hand but seldom consulted.

Dag Hammarskjöld (1905–1961)
Swedish statesman and humanitarian

Pass It On List

❑ _____

❑ _____

❑ _____

❑ _____

❑ _____

30
My Gratitude Journal

People, events, and activities for which I am thoughtfully and specifically grateful this week:

1. _____

2. _____

3. _____

4. _____

5. _____

My IOTAs

Ideas, Observations, Thoughts, and *Affirmations* I want to record and remember for future consideration:

_____

_____

_____

_____

_____

Humble yourselves before the Lord,
and he will lift you up.

—James 4:10

I am like a little pencil in his hand.
That is all.
He does the thinking.
He does the writing.
The pencil has nothing to do with it.
The pencil has only to be allowed to be used.

Mother Teresa (1910–1997)
Missionary to the poor in Calcutta, India

Pass It On List

❏ _____

❏ _____

❏ _____

❏ _____

❏ _____

31
My Gratitude Journal

People, events, and activities for which I am thoughtfully and specifically grateful this week:

1. _____

2. _____

3. _____

4. _____

5. _____

My IOTAs

Ideas, Observations, Thoughts, and *Affirmations* I want to record and remember for future consideration:

_____

_____

_____

_____

_____

Each one must give as he has made up his mind,
not reluctantly or under compulsion,
for God loves a cheerful giver.

—2 Corinthians 9:7 (ESV)

As we express our gratitude,
we must never forget that
the highest appreciation
is not to utter words,
but to live by them.

—John F. Kennedy (1917–1963)
35th President of the United States

Pass It On List

❑ _____

❑ _____

❑ _____

❑ _____

❑ _____

32
My Gratitude Journal

People, events, and activities for which I am thoughtfully and specifically grateful this week:

1. _____

2. _____

3. _____

4. _____

5. _____

My IOTAs

Ideas, Observations, Thoughts, and *Affirmations* I want to record and remember for future consideration:

_____

_____

_____

_____

_____

Ask and it will be given to you;
seek and you will find;
knock and the door will be opened to you.

—Matthew 7:7

If there is something to gain
and nothing to lose by asking,
by all means, ask!

—W. Clement Stone (1902–2002)
American businessman and philanthropist

Pass It On List

❑ _____

❑ _____

❑ _____

❑ _____

❑ _____

33
My Gratitude Journal

People, events, and activities for which I am thoughtfully and specifically grateful this week:

1. _____

2. _____

3. _____

4. _____

5. _____

My IOTAs

Ideas, Observations, Thoughts, and *Affirmations* I want to record and remember for future consideration:

_____

_____

_____

_____

_____

He who guards his mouth and his tongue
keeps himself from calamity.

—Proverbs 21:23

Knowing when to keep your mouth shut
is invariably more important
than opening it at the right time.

—Malcom Forbes (1919–1990)
American publisher

Pass It On List

❑ _____

❑ _____

❑ _____

❑ _____

❑ _____

34
My Gratitude Journal

People, events, and activities for which I am thoughtfully and specifically grateful this week:

1. _____

2. _____

3. _____

4. _____

5. _____

My IOTAs

Ideas, Observations, Thoughts, and *Affirmations* I want to record and remember for future consideration:

_____

_____

_____

_____

_____

Commit to the Lord whatever you do
and your plans will succeed.

—Proverbs 16:3

How can you build a life worth living
if you don't have a plan?

Pass It On List

- [ ] _____
- [ ] _____
- [ ] _____
- [ ] _____
- [ ] _____

35
My Gratitude Journal

People, events, and activities for which I am thoughtfully and specifically grateful this week:

1. _____

2. _____

3. _____

4. _____

5. _____

My IOTAs

Ideas, Observations, Thoughts, and *Affirmations* I want to record and remember for future consideration:

_____

_____

_____

_____

_____

Be kind and compassionate to one another,
forgiving each other, just as in Christ
God forgave you.

—Ephesians 4:32

Those who cannot forgive others
break the bridge
over which they themselves must pass.

—Confucius (551–479 BC)
Chinese philosopher

Pass It On List

☐ _____

☐ _____

☐ _____

☐ _____

☐ _____

36
My Gratitude Journal

People, events, and activities for which I am thoughtfully and specifically grateful this week:

1. _____

2. _____

3. _____

4. _____

5. _____

My IOTAs

Ideas, Observations, Thoughts, and *Affirmations* I want to record and remember for future consideration:

_____

_____

_____

_____

_____

It is more blessed to give than to receive.

—Acts 20:35b

You make a living by what you get.
You make a life by what you give.

—Sir Winston Churchill (1874–1965)
British Prime Minister

Pass It On List

❑ _____

❑ _____

❑ _____

❑ _____

❑ _____

37
My Gratitude Journal

People, events, and activities for which I am thoughtfully and specifically grateful this week:

1. _____

2. _____

3. _____

4. _____

5. _____

My IOTAs

Ideas, Observations, Thoughts, and *Affirmations* I want to record and remember for future consideration:

_____

_____

_____

_____

_____

And now these three remain: faith, hope and love.
But the greatest of these is love.

—1 Corinthians 13:13

When the power of love
conquers the love of power,
you will know peace, joy, and contentment.

Pass It On List

❑ _____

❑ _____

❑ _____

❑ _____

❑ _____

38
My Gratitude Journal

People, events, and activities for which I am thoughtfully and specifically grateful this week:

1. _____

2. _____

3. _____

4. _____

5. _____

My IOTAs

Ideas, Observations, Thoughts, and *Affirmations* I want to record and remember for future consideration:

_____

_____

_____

_____

_____

All hard work brings a profit,
but mere talk leads only to poverty.

—Proverbs 14:23

When the time of need arrives,
the time for preparation is past.

Pass It On List

❑ _____

❑ _____

❑ _____

❑ _____

❑ _____

39
My Gratitude Journal

People, events, and activities for which I am thoughtfully and specifically grateful this week:

1. _____

2. _____

3. _____

4. _____

5. _____

My IOTAs

Ideas, Observations, Thoughts, and *Affirmations* I want to record and remember for future consideration:

_____

_____

_____

_____

_____

You may say to yourself,
"My power and the strength of my hands
have produced this wealth for me."
But remember the Lord your God,
for it is he who gives you
the ability to produce wealth.

—Deuteronomy 8:17–18b

Thanksgiving invites God
to bestow a second benefit.

—Robert Herrick (1591–1674)
English poet

Pass It On List

❑ _____

❑ _____

❑ _____

❑ _____

❑ _____

40
My Gratitude Journal

People, events, and activities for which I am thoughtfully and specifically grateful this week:

1. _____

2. _____

3. _____

4. _____

5. _____

My IOTAs

Ideas, Observations, Thoughts, and *Affirmations* I want to record and remember for future consideration:

_____

_____

_____

_____

_____

The more the words,
the less the meaning, and
how does that profit anyone?

—Ecclesiastes 6:11

When you don't know what you're talking about,
it's hard to know when you're finished.

—Tom Smothers
American comedian

Pass It On List

❑ _____

❑ _____

❑ _____

❑ _____

❑ _____

41
My Gratitude Journal

People, events, and activities for which I am thoughtfully and specifically grateful this week:

1. _____

2. _____

3. _____

4. _____

5. _____

My IOTAs

Ideas, Observations, Thoughts, and *Affirmations* I want to record and remember for future consideration:

_____

_____

_____

_____

_____

The prayer of a righteous man
is powerful and effective.

—James 5:16b

Pray as though everything depended on God.
Work as though everything depended on you.

—St. Augustine (354–430)
Roman Catholic saint

Pass It On List

❑ _____

❑ _____

❑ _____

❑ _____

❑ _____

42
My Gratitude Journal

People, events, and activities for which I am thoughtfully and specifically grateful this week:

1. _____

2. _____

3. _____

4. _____

5. _____

My IOTAs

Ideas, Observations, Thoughts, and *Affirmations* I want to record and remember for future consideration:

_____

_____

_____

_____

_____

And whatever you do, whether in word or deed,
do it all in the name of the Lord Jesus,
giving thanks to God the Father through him.

—Colossians 3:17

Besides the noble art of getting things done,
there is the noble art of leaving things undone.
The wisdom of life consists
in the elimination of nonessentials.

—Lin Yutang (1895–1976)
Chinese writer

Pass It On List

❑ _____

❑ _____

❑ _____

❑ _____

❑ _____

43
My Gratitude Journal

People, events, and activities for which I am thoughtfully and specifically grateful this week:

1. _____

2. _____

3. _____

4. _____

5. _____

My IOTAs

Ideas, Observations, Thoughts, and *Affirmations* I want to record and remember for future consideration:

_____

_____

_____

_____

_____

Have nothing to do
with godless myths and old wives' tales;
rather train yourself to be godly.

—1 Timothy 4:7

There is no chance, no destiny, no fate
that can circumvent, hinder or control
the firm resolve of a determined soul.

—Ella Wheeler Wilcox (1850–1919)
American poet

Pass It On List

- ❏ _____
- ❏ _____
- ❏ _____
- ❏ _____
- ❏ _____

44
My Gratitude Journal

People, events, and activities for which I am thoughtfully and specifically grateful this week:

1. _____

2. _____

3. _____

4. _____

5. _____

My IOTAs

Ideas, Observations, Thoughts, and *Affirmations* I want to record and remember for future consideration:

_____

_____

_____

_____

_____

...the Lord searches every heart and
understands every motive behind the thoughts.
If you seek him, he will be found by you.

—1 Chronicles 28:9b

If you are not guided by God,
you will be guided by someone or something else.
—Eric Liddell (1902–1945)
Scottish athlete and Christian missionary

Pass It On List

❑ _____

❑ _____

❑ _____

❑ _____

❑ _____

45
My Gratitude Journal

People, events, and activities for which I am thoughtfully and specifically grateful this week:

1. _____

2. _____

3. _____

4. _____

5. _____

My IOTAs

Ideas, Observations, Thoughts, and *Affirmations* I want to record and remember for future consideration:

_____

_____

_____

_____

_____

_____

Remember this: Whoever sows sparingly
will also reap sparingly,
and whoever sows generously
will also reap generously.

—1 Corinthians 9:6

The future depends
on what we do in the present.
—Mahatma Gandhi (1869–1948)
Indian spiritual leader and humanitarian

Pass It On List

❑ _____

❑ _____

❑ _____

❑ _____

❑ _____

46
My Gratitude Journal

People, events, and activities for which I am thoughtfully and specifically grateful this week:

1. _____

2. _____

3. _____

4. _____

5. _____

My IOTAs

Ideas, Observations, Thoughts, and *Affirmations* I want to record and remember for future consideration:

_____

_____

_____

_____

_____

He has made everything beautiful in its time.
He has also set eternity in the hearts of men;
yet they cannot fathom what God has done
from beginning to end.

—Ecclesiastes 3:11

God, grant me the serenity
to accept the things I cannot change,
the courage to change the things I can,
and the wisdom to know the difference.

—Richard Niebuhr (1892–1971)
American theologian

Pass It On List

❏ _____

❏ _____

❏ _____

❏ _____

❏ _____

47
My Gratitude Journal

People, events, and activities for which I am thoughtfully and specifically grateful this week:

1. _____

2. _____

3. _____

4. _____

5. _____

My IOTAs

Ideas, Observations, Thoughts, and *Affirmations* I want to record and remember for future consideration:

_____

_____

_____

_____

_____

Seek ye first the kingdom of God and
His righteousness, and all these things,
shall be added unto you.

—Matthew 6:33 (KJV)

A career is what you are paid to do.
A calling is what you were made to do.

—Dr. Howard G. Hendricks
Christian educator and author

Pass It On List

❏ _____

❏ _____

❏ _____

❏ _____

❏ _____

48
My Gratitude Journal

People, events, and activities for which I am thoughtfully and specifically grateful this week:

1. _____

2. _____

3. _____

4. _____

5. _____

My IOTAs

Ideas, Observations, Thoughts, and *Affirmations* I want to record and remember for future consideration:

_____

_____

_____

_____

_____

There is no fear in love.
But perfect love drives out fear,
because fear has to do with punishment.

—1 John 4:18a

It is not because things are difficult
that we dare not venture.
It is because we dare not venture
that things are difficult.

—Lucius Annaceus Seneca (4 BC–65 AD)
Roman philosopher

Pass It On List

❑ _____

❑ _____

❑ _____

❑ _____

❑ _____

49
My Gratitude Journal

People, events, and activities for which I am thoughtfully and specifically grateful this week:

1. _____

2. _____

3. _____

4. _____

5. _____

My IOTAs

Ideas, Observations, Thoughts, and *Affirmations* I want to record and remember for future consideration:

_____

_____

_____

_____

_____

A good name is more desirable than great riches;
to be esteemed is better than silver or gold.

—Proverbs 22:1

There are men and women
who make the world better
just by being the kind of people they are.

—John W. Gardner (1912–2002)
American educator and author

Pass It On List

❑ _____

❑ _____

❑ _____

❑ _____

❑ _____

50
My Gratitude Journal

People, events, and activities for which I am thoughtfully and specifically grateful this week:

1. _____

2. _____

3. _____

4. _____

5. _____

My IOTAs

Ideas, Observations, Thoughts, and *Affirmations* I want to record and remember for future consideration:

_____

_____

_____

_____

_____

Each of you should look
not only to your own interests,
but also to the interests of others

—Philippians 2:4

Life becomes harder for us
when we live for others but
it also becomes richer and happier.

—Albert Schweitzer (1875–1965)
German medical missionary

Pass It On List

❏ _____

❏ _____

❏ _____

❏ _____

❏ _____

51
My Gratitude Journal

People, events, and activities for which I am thoughtfully and specifically grateful this week:

1. _____

2. _____

3. _____

4. _____

5. _____

My IOTAs

Ideas, Observations, Thoughts, and *Affirmations* I want to record and remember for future consideration:

_____

_____

_____

_____

_____

Call unto me and I will answer thee
and show thee great and mighty things
which thou knowest not.

—Jeremiah 33:3 (KJV)

Prayer is the soul's sincere desire,
uttered or unexpressed.

James Montgomery (1771–1854)
British editor and poet

Pass It On List

❏ _____

❏ _____

❏ _____

❏ _____

❏ _____

52
My Gratitude Journal

People, events, and activities for which I am thoughtfully and specifically grateful this week:

1. _____

2. _____

3. _____

4. _____

5. _____

My IOTAs

Ideas, Observations, Thoughts, and *Affirmations* I want to record and remember for future consideration:

_____

_____

_____

_____

_____

And we know that in all things
God works for the good
of those who love him,
who have been called
according to his purpose.

—Romans 8:28

Faith keeps the person that keeps the faith.
Mother Teresa (1910–1997)
Missionary to the poor in Calcutta, India

Pass It On List

❑ _____

❑ _____

❑ _____

❑ _____

❑ _____

One of the most tragic things I know about human nature
is that all of us tend to put off living.
We are all dreaming of some magical rose garden
over the horizon—instead of enjoying the roses
blooming outside our windows today.[1]

Learn to Live!

Life is lived forward but understood backward.[2]

We're *smart* when we learn from personal experience; we're *wise* when we learn from the experience of someone else.

The primary emphasis of this book is to give you guidance in learning to live a better, more satisfying life. Each chapter has been designed to encourage you to develop habits that will enable you to live each day with a grateful heart.

It is critically important that our brains constantly receive "food" that will nourish both the mind and the heart. As you study and memorize the fifty-two Bible verses and think about the positive thoughts and quotations presented in each weekly assignment, you will see yourself becoming a more optimistic and generous person.

Since it is often more economical and less painful to learn from the experiences of others, this final chapter is provided as a handy reference to wisdom from people who have traveled a different path in life than the path you're traveling.

Bite-sized lessons highlighting attributes that contribute to maximum success, satisfaction, and contentment in life are presented on the following pages. Carefully review each category and consider how this collective wisdom can be used to improve your life and the lives of those you love.

Grab a highlighter and read on!

Lessons on Achievement

The value of life lies not in the length of days, but in the use we make of them; a man may live long yet live very little.

—Michel Eyguem de Montaigne (1533–1592)
French Renaissance essayist

Some people have greatness thrust upon them. Very few have excellence thrust upon them...they achieve it. They do not achieve it unwittingly by doing what comes naturally and they don't stumble into it in the course of amusing themselves. All excellence involves discipline and tenacity of purpose.

—John W. Gardner (1912–2002)
American educator and author

Until significant thought is linked to a significant goal, there can be no significant accomplishment.

—J. Carl Newell
American businessman and author

You must get good at one of two things...sowing in the spring or begging in the fall.

—Jim Rohn
American philosopher and author

It is the nature of man to rise to greatness if greatness is expected of him.

—John Steinbeck (1902–1968)
American author

Talk doesn't cook the rice.

—Chinese proverb

Unless a capacity for thinking is accompanied with a capacity for action, a superior mind exists in torture.

—Benedetto Croce (1866–1952)
Italian philosopher

There is only one thing that makes a dream impossible to achieve: the fear of failure.

—Paulo Coelho
Brazilian writer in *The Alchemist*

Ability determines what you're capable of doing. *Motivation* determines what you will attempt. *Attitude* determines the measure of success you will achieve.

—J. Carl Newell
American businessman and author

Lessons on Attitude

The greatest discovery of my generation is that human beings can alter their lives by altering their attitudes of mind.

—William James (1842–1910)
American psychologist

What it lies in our power to do, it lies in our power to not do.

—Aristotle (384–322 BC)
Greek educator, philosopher and author

Nothing can stop the man with the right mental attitude from achieving his goal; nothing on earth can help the man with the wrong mental attitude.

—Thomas Jefferson (1743–1826)
3rd President of the United States

The people who get on in this world are the people who get up and look for the circumstances they want and if they can't find them, make them.

—George Bernard Shaw (1856–1950)
Irish dramatist and playwright

Keep your face to the sunshine and you cannot see the shadows.

—Helen Keller (1880–1960)
American author and inspirational role model

Shallow men believe in luck; strong men believe in cause and effect.

—Ralph Waldo Emerson (1803–1882)
American poet and philosopher

Things turn out best for the people who make the best of the way things turn out.

—John Wooden
Legendary UCLA and Hall of Fame basketball coach

Attitude and success are Siamese twins.

—J. Carl Newell
American businessman and author

Be enthusiastic. Every occasion is an opportunity to do good.
—Russell H. Conwell (1843–1925)
American minister and author

It is difficult to say what is impossible, for the dream of yesterday is the hope of today and the reality of tomorrow.
—Robert Goddard (1882–1945)
American scientist

The clearest sign of wisdom is continued cheerfulness.
—Michel Eyguem de Montaigne (1533–1592)
French Renaissance essayist

Lessons on Character

Character is the sum total of our everyday choices.
—Anonymous

Character is like a tree and reputation like its shadow. The shadow is what we think of it; the tree is the real thing.
—Abraham Lincoln (1809–1865)
16th President of the United States

What this country needs is dirtier fingernails and cleaner minds.
—Will Rogers (1879–1935)
American cowboy, actor and philosopher

The ultimate measure of a man is not where he stands in moments of comfort and convenience, but where he stands at times of challenges and controversy.

—Dr. Martin Luther King, Jr. (1929–1968)
American civil rights leader

Be more concerned with your character than your reputation because your character is what you really are; your reputation is merely what others think you are.

—John Wooden, Legendary UCLA and
Hall of Fame basketball coach

The reputation of a thousand years may be determined by the conduct of one hour.

—Japanese Proverb

Integrity is doing the right thing even when no one sees you.

—Unknown

Words to live by are just words, unless we live by them.

—Unknown

People of character do the right thing, not because they think it will change the world but because they refuse to be changed by the world.

—Michael Josephson
American ethicist

Would you buy a used car from yourself?

—Sparky (George L.) Anderson
Hall of Fame baseball manager

Lessons on Choice

Destiny is not a matter of chance, it is a matter of choice; it is not a thing to be waited for, it is a thing to be achieved.

—William Jennings Bryan (1860–1925)
American orator and politician

We must make the choices that enable us to fulfill the deepest capacities of our real selves.

—Thomas Merton (1915–1968)
French-born American poet and author

All of life is but a mass of small choices—practical, emotional and intellectual—systematically organized for our greatness or grief.

—William James (1842–1910)
American psychologist

If fate throws a knife at you, there are two ways of catching it—by the blade or by the handle. Choose carefully.

—Oriental proverb

My future starts when I wake up every morning. Every day, I find something creative to do with my life.

—Miles Davis (1926–1991)
American jazz musician

Choose your companions before you choose your road.

—Proverb from The Moors of North Africa

There is a choice you have to make, in everything you do. So keep in mind that in the end, the choice you make, makes you.

—John Wooden
Legendary UCLA and Hall of Fame basketball coach

One can choose to go back toward safety or forward toward growth. Growth must be chosen again and again; fear must be overcome again and again.

—Abraham Maslow (1908–1970)
American psychologist and educator

You have brains in your head. You have feet in your shoes. You can steer yourself any direction you choose.

—Theodor S. Geisel (Dr. Seuss) (1904–1991)
American writer and illustrator

The greatest weapon against stress is our ability to choose one thought over another.

—William James (1842–1910)
American psychologist

Lessons on Courage

Only those who will risk going too far can possibly find out how far one can go.

—T. S. Eliot (1888–1965)
American poet

Life shrinks or expands in proportion to one's courage.

—Adlai Stevenson (1900–1965)
American diplomat and politician

Do the thing you fear, and the death of fear is certain.

—Ralph Waldo Emerson (1803–1882)
American writer and philosopher

Courage is contagious. When a brave man takes a stand, the spines of others are stiffened.

—Billy Graham
American evangelist

Don't be afraid to take a big step if one is indicated. You can't cross a chasm in two small jumps.

—David Lloyd George (1863–1945)
British Prime Minister

Courage is not the absence of fear, but the capacity to act despite our fears.

—John McCain
Viet Nam POW, United States Senator

To fight a bull when you are not scared is nothing. And to not fight a bull when you are scared is nothing. But to fight a bull when you are scared is something.

—Unknown

Far better it is to dare mighty things, to win glorious triumphs, even though checkered by failure, than to take rank with those poor spirits who neither enjoy much nor suffer much, because they live in the gray twilight that knows not victory nor defeat.

—Theodore Roosevelt (1858–1919)
26th President of the United States

He who has a *why* to live can bear any *how*.

—Viktor Frankl (1905–1997)
Austrian physician, psychoanalyst and author

Lessons on Ethics

Moral excellence comes about as a result of habit. We become just by doing just acts, temperate by doing temperate acts, brave by doing brave acts.

—Aristotle (384–322 BC)
Greek philosopher

The truth of the matter is that you always know the right thing to do. The hard part is doing it.

—H. Norman Schwarzkopf, Jr.
General, U. S. Army (Retired)

When men no longer fear God, they transgress His laws without hesitation. The fear of consequences is no deterrent when the fear of God is gone.

—A. W. Tozer (1897–1963)
American minister

Example is not the main thing in influencing others. It is the only thing.

—Albert Schweitzer (1875–1965)
German medical missionary

Virtue, though in rags, will keep me warm.

—John Dryden (1631–1700)
English dramatist

Ours is a world of nuclear giants and ethical infants. We have grasped the mystery of the atom and rejected the Sermon on the Mount.

—Omar N. Bradley (1893–1981)
General of the Army, United States Army

Honesty doesn't exist in degrees. Different lies carry different consequences.

—Unknown

Honor is better than honors.

—Abraham Lincoln (1809–1865)
16th President of the United States

The measure of a man's character is what he would do if he knew he never would be found out.

—Thomas Babington (1800–1859)
British poet, historian and politician

Expedients are for the hour, but principles are for the ages.

—Henry Ward Beecher (1813–1887)
American clergyman

Lessons on Failure

I cannot give you the formula for success, but I can give you the formula for failure, which is: Try to please everybody.

—Herbert Bayard Swope (1882–1958)
American journalist and editor

Ninety-nine percent of failures come from people who have the habit of making excuses.

—George Washington Carver (1864–1943)
American educator and scientist

Never confuse a single defeat with a final defeat.

—F. Scott Fitzgerald (1896–1940)
American novelist

Failure is only an opportunity to begin again more intelligently.

—Henry Ford (1863–1947)
American industrialist and inventor

Errors and mistakes are the necessary steps in the learning process; once they have served their purpose, they should be forgotten.

—Vince Lombardi (1913–1970)
Hall of Fame Football Coach

The price of success is perseverance. The price of failure comes cheaper.

—Robert Half (1919–2001)
Founder, Robert Half International

When looking for a reason why things go wrong, never rule out sheer stupidity.

—Unknown

Failure is an event, not a person.

—Zig Ziglar
American motivational guru

Indecision and delays are the parents of failure.

—George Canning (1770–1827)
British statesman

I've failed over and over and over again in my life. And that is why I succeed.

—Michael Jordan
NBA basketball player and businessman

It doesn't matter how much milk you spill as long as you don't lose your cow.

—Texas proverb

Lessons on Gratitude

He is a wise man who does not grieve for the things which he has not, but rejoices for those which he has.

—Epictetus (55–135)
Greek philosopher

A thankful heart is not only the greatest virtue, but the parent of all other virtues.

—Marcus Tullius Cicero (106–43 BC)
Roman statesman and philosopher

He who gives when he is asked has waited too long.

—Lucius Annaeus Seneca (4 BC–65 AD)
Roman statesman and philosopher

Kind words can be short and easy to speak, but their echoes are truly endless.

—Mother Teresa (1910–1997)
Missionary to India, Nobel Peace Prize winner

When I was young, I admired clever people. Now that I am old, I admire kind people.

—Abraham Joseph Heschel (1907–1972)
Hasidic Jewish scholar and author

Kindness is loving people more than they deserve.

—Joseph Joubert (1754–1824)
French philosopher and essayist

When eating a fruit, think of the person who planted the tree.

—Vietnamese proverb

You cannot do a kindness too soon, for you never know how soon it will be too late.

—Ralph Waldo Emerson (1803–1882)
American writer and philosopher

A generous man will prosper; he who refreshes others will himself be refreshed.

—Proverbs 11:25

If I keep a green bough in my heart, the singing bird will come.

—Chinese proverb

*If someone paid you ten dollars for every kind word you ever spoke
and collected five dollars for every unkind word,
would you be rich or poor?*

Lessons on Happiness

It is the chiefest point of happiness that a man is willing to be what he is.

—Desiderius Erasmus (1466–1536)
German humanist

Happiness is like a butterfly. When pursued, it is always just out of reach. But if you will sit quietly, it will come and light upon your shoulder.

—Robert Louis Stevenson (1850–1894)
Scottish writer

Success is not the key to happiness. Happiness is the key to success. If you love what you are doing, you will be successful.

—Albert Schweitzer (1875–1965)
German medical missionary

People are lonely because they build walls instead of bridges.

—W. E. Channing (1780–1842)
American minister and abolitionist

We must be doing something to be happy. Action is no less necessary to us than thought.

—William Hazlitt (1778–1830)
English essayist

Action may not always bring happiness, but there is no happiness without action.

—Benjamin Disraeli (1804–1881)
British statesman and Prime Minister

Happiness is someone to love, something to do, and something to hope for.

—Chinese proverb

The Constitution only guarantees the American people the right to pursue happiness. You have to catch it yourself.

—Benjamin Franklin (1706–1790)
American statesman and inventor

The happiness of your life depends on the quality of your thoughts.

—Marcus Aurelius (121–180)

Emperor of Rome

Success is getting what you want. Happiness is wanting what you get.

—Dave Gardner (1926–1983)

American humorist

Lessons on Relationships

Those who cannot forgive others break the bridge over which they themselves must pass.

—Confucius (551–479 BC)

Chinese philosopher

Life becomes harder when we live for others but it also becomes richer and happier.

—Albert Schweitzer (1875–1965)

German medical missionary

There is so much good in the worst of us, and so much bad in the best of us, that it behooves all of us not to talk about the rest of us.

—Robert Louis Stevenson (1850–1894)

Scottish writer

Trust men and they will be true to you; treat them greatly and they will show themselves great.

—Ralph Waldo Emerson (1803–1882)

American writer and philosopher

Why must we have enough memory to recall to the tiniest detail of what has happened to us, and not have enough to remember how many times we have told it to the same person?

—Francois de La Rochefoucauld (1613–1680)
French author and moralist

At some time, our inner fire goes out. It is then burst into flame by an encounter with another human being. We should all be thankful for those people who rekindle the inner spirit.

—Albert Schweitzer (1875–1965)
German medical missionary

We find comfort among those who agree with us and growth among those who don't.

—Frank A. Clark

Praise is well, compliment is well, but affection—that is the last and final and most precious reward that any man can win, whether by character or achievement.

—Mark Twain (1835–1910)
American writer and humorist

I like pigs. Dogs look up to us. Cats look down on us. Pigs treat us as equals.

—Sir Winston Churchill (1874–1965)
British Prime Minister

Lessons on Responsibility

The price of greatness is responsibility.

—Sir Winston Churchill (1874–1965)
British Prime Minister

It's a bad carpenter who quarrels with his tools. It is a bad general who blames his men for faulty workmanship.

—Mahatma Gandhi (1869–1948)
Indian spiritual leader and humanitarian

It is not only for what we do that we are held responsible, but also for what we do not do.

—John Baptiste Moliére (1622–1673)
French playwright

You cannot escape the responsibility of tomorrow by evading it today.

—Abraham Lincoln (1809–1865)
16th President of the United States

Man must cease attributing his problems to his environment, and learn again to exercise his will and his personal responsibility.

—Albert Schweitzer (1875–1965)
German medical missionary

Faced with crisis, the man of character falls back on himself. He imposes his own stamp of action, takes responsibility for it and makes it his own.

—Charles de Gaulle (1890–1970)
French general, president, and statesman

I believe life is a series of near-misses. A lot of what we ascribe to luck is not luck at all. It's seizing the day and accepting responsibility for your future.

—Howard Schultz, American businessman
Founder of Starbucks Coffee

Nothing strengthens the judgment and quickens the conscience like individual responsibility.

—Elizabeth Cady Stanton (1815–1902)
American writer, editor, and activist

Every individual has a young person and
an old person living within them.
It is the young person's responsibility
to take care of the old person.

Lessons on Success

If A is success in life, then A equals x plus y plus z. Work is x; y is play; and z is keeping your mouth shut.

—Albert Einstein (1879–1955)
German-born theoretical physicist

Success is peace of mind which is a direct result of self-satisfaction in knowing you did your best to become the best that you are capable of becoming.

—John Wooden
Legendary UCLA and Hall of Fame basketball coach

Success is going from failure to failure without loss of enthusiasm.

—Sir Winston Churchill (1874–1965)
British Prime Minister

The world is divided into people who do things and people who get the credit. Try, if you can, to be in the first class. There's far less competition.

—Dwight W. Morrow (1873–1931)
American banker and politician

The line between failure and success is so fine that we scarcely know when we pass it; so fine that we are often on the line and do not know it.

—Elbert Hubbard (1856–1915)
American philosopher and author

There are no secrets to success. It is the result of preparation, hard work and learning from failure.

—Colin L. Powell
General, U. S. Army (Retired), Secretary of State

The secret of getting ahead is getting started. The secret of getting started is breaking your complex, overwhelming tasks into small manageable tasks, and then starting on the first one.

—Mark Twain (1835–1910)
American writer and humorist

Don't confuse fame with success. Madonna is one; Helen Keller is the other.

—Erma Bombeck (1927–1996)
American humorist and columnist

Don't worry about failure. Worry about all the success you miss because you didn't even try!

—J. Carl Newell
American businessman and author

Lessons on Thinking

A man's life is what his thoughts make of it.

—Marcus Aurelius (121–180 AD)
Emperor of Rome

Our best friends and our worst enemies are our thoughts.

—Dr. Frank Crane
American essayist and philosopher

Two percent of the people think; three percent of the people think they think and ninety-five percent of the people would rather die than think.

—George Bernard Shaw (1856–1950)
Irish dramatist and playwright

As he thinks, so he is; as he continues to think, so he remains.

—James Allen (1864–1912)
British author

Great men are those who see that thoughts rule the world.

—Ralph Waldo Emerson (1803–1882)
American writer and philosopher

They *can* because they *think* they can.

—Virgil (70 BC–19 BC)
Roman poet

Except our own thoughts, there is nothing absolutely in our power.

—René Descartes (1596–1650)
French philosopher and mathematician

It is the mark of an educated mind to be able to entertain a thought without accepting it.

—Aristotle (384–322 BC)
Greek educator, philosopher and author

Commit thy works unto the Lord, and thy thoughts shall be established.

—The Bible
Proverbs 16:3, *King James Version*

The greatest weapon against stress is our ability to choose one thought over another.

—William James (1842–1910)
American psychologist and philosopher

Keep your mind off the things you don't want by keeping it on the things you do want.

—W. Clement Stone (1902–2002)
American businessman and philanthropist

We Want to Hear from You!

Has this book helped you? I would greatly appreciate your comments regarding *The Gratitude Attitude.* If this book has helped improve your life, I would love to hear about it.

Can you help me? I constantly have need of personal illustrations and inspirational stories as I seek to help folks learn how to have a better life. Tell me how God has helped someone you know overcome adversity and share ideas you believe can help others have a better quality life.

Your feedback is very important to me.

Contact me at jcarl@mybestfuture.com

or

J. Carl Newell
Best Quest, Inc.
1911 Grayson Highway, Suite 8–222
Grayson, GA 30017
Visit our website at www.mybestfuture.com

I look forward to hearing from you!

End Notes

Change Your World

1. George Washington Carver (1864–1943) was an agricultural chemist who worked tirelessly to discover ways to make America's farmland more productive. The epitaph inscribed on his tombstone reflects the humility of his life: "He could have added fortune to fame, but caring for neither, he found happiness and honor in being helpful to the world."

2. Hal David is an American lyricist and songwriter. Much of his work has been in collaboration with award-winning composer Burt Bacharach. His song *Raindrops Keep Fallin' on My Head* won an Academy Award as the score for the movie *Butch Cassidy and the Sundance Kid.*

3. From a news release titled *Americans Struggle With Religion's Role At Home and Abroad,* by The Pew Forum on Religion & Public Life, March 20, 2002.

4. An international group of scientists at the *Avoiding Dangerous Climate Change* conference in Exeter, United Kingdom (February 2005) concluded that unless "urgent and strenuous mitigation actions" are taken in the next twenty years, it is almost certain that by 2050, global temperatures will have risen to between 0.9 and 3.6°F above current levels. Source: www.wikipedia.org

5. Robert Burns' dirge *Man Was Made to Mourn* includes this phrase: "Man's inhumanity to man make countless thousands mourn." Robert Burns (1759–1796) was a poet and lyricist and is regarded as the national poet of Scotland.

6. Poem: *The Cold Within* was written by James Patrick Kinney during the 1960s and rejected by *The Saturday Evening Post* as being "too controversial" for the times. Reprinted by permission.

7. Sir John Marks Templeton is an American-born naturalized British citizen who is a highly successful pioneer of globally diversified mutual funds and extremely interested in spiritual endeavors. This information is from his book *Worldwide Laws of Life* (Radnor, PA: Templeton Foundation Press, 1997), pp. 10, 11.

8. John W. Gardner (1912–2002) was a distinguished educator, author, and presidential advisor. This quote is from his book *Living, Leading and the American Dream* (San Francisco: Jossey-Bass, 2003) p. 45.

9. John Donne (1572–1631) was an English poet and preacher. This quote is from his *Meditation XVII* in his book *Devotions Upon Emergent Occasions*.

10. Karl Menninger (1893–1990) was an American psychiatrist and author. This quote is from his book *The Human Mind* (New York: Alfred A. Knopf, 1945).

11. Grantland Rice (1880–1954) was an American sportswriter. This quote is from his 1941 poem *Alumnus Football*.

Light Your Torch

1. Jack London (1876–1916) was an American author. One of the most successful writers in America during the early 20th century, London wrote more than fifty books including *The Call of the Wild* and *White Fang*.

2. George Bernard Shaw (1856–1950) was an Irish author, playwright and socialist. This quote is from *Man and Superman* (New York: Penguin, 1950), preface.

3. William James (1842–1910) was a pioneering psychologist and philosopher during the 19th century. His 1200 page masterwork, *The Principles*

of Psychology (1890), influenced generations of thinkers in Europe and America.

4. Sir Francis Bacon (1561–1626) was an English philosopher, essayist, and statesman.

5. Melody Beattie is a journalist and best-selling author of fourteen books including *Codependent No More* and *Language of Letting Go.* Visit www.melodybeattie.com for more information about Melody's work.

6. Aldous Huxley (1894–1963) was a British writer, author of *Brave New World.* This quote is from a lecture given toward the end of his life. Source: *The Power of Kindness* by Piero Ferrucci (New York: Penguin Group, 2006), p. 8.

7. Mark Twain (1835–1910) was the pen name of Samuel Langhorne Clemens, a famous humorist, novelist, writer, and lecturer. Mark Twain wrote an impressive number of fiction and non-fiction books including *The Adventures of Tom Sawyer, The Adventures of Huckleberry Finn,* and *The Prince and the Pauper.*

8. Lord Byron (George Gordon Noel Byron) (1788–1824), English poet, satirist, and member of the House of Lords.

9. Mark Albion, American author as quoted in *Motto* magazine, 2006 premiere issue.

10. Examples of Dr. Wall's classroom assignment are provided courtesy of James S. Huggins. See www.JamesSHuggins.com for additional information.

11. Dr. Chuck Wall is the author of *The Kindness Collection* and co-author with Kimberly Walton of *Selling Lemonade for Free.* Visit www.kindnessinc.org for additional information.

12. Ralph Waldo Emerson (1803–1882), was an American essayist and philosopher, as well as one of America's most influential thinkers and writers.

13. John W. Gardner, *Living, Leading and the American Dream* (San Francisco: Jossey-Bass, 2003) p. 37.

14. Poem: *The Bridge Builder* was written by Will Allen Dromgoole (1860–1934), a writer and journalist who had a thirty year career with the *Nashville* (TN) *Banner*. Her novel *The Island of the Beautiful* was on the 1911 best-seller list. During World War I, Dromgoole was a warrant officer in the United States Navy, lecturing to sailors on patriotic topics. She was perhaps the first woman to serve in the United States Navy.

The Gratitude Attitude

1. M. Walter Levine, an American entrepreneur was diagnosed with multiple myeloma, melanoma, and subsequently, bladder cancer in 1991. Since that time, he has been actively involved—personally and financially—in encouraging cancer patients and working to ensure that the best possible care is available to them. Commenting on his current good health, Mr. Levine says, "I think God gave me a gift and He's allowing me to just give it back." Source: WestportMinuteman.com, article by Melissa L. Shaw, March 16, 2006.

2. Paul Speicher (1893–1952) was an American publisher, author, and educator.

3. Source: Gary DeMar, *America's Heritage*, (Coral Ridge Ministries: Fort Lauderdale, FL, 2002) p. 10. Writing an 1892 ruling in: *The Church of the Holy Trinity vs. United States,* David J. Brewer, associate justice of the Supreme Court of the United States declared that America was a Christian nation from its earliest days. Associate Justice Brewer concluded that Americans "…are a religious people. This is historically true. From the discovery of this continent to the present hour, there is a single voice making this affirmation."

4. From a news release titled *Americans Struggle With Religion's Role At Home and Abroad*, by The Pew Forum on Religion & Public Life, March 20, 2002.

5. Source: *Newsweek/Beliefnet Poll Results*, August 2005 where Americans were asked what they believe and how they practice their faith.

6. Harry Blamires, British educator and author. Source: *The Christian Mind*, first published in 1963 by S. P. C. K. Holy Trinity Church, Marleybone Road, London, England.

The Gratitude Journal

1. Annelies Marie "Anne" Frank (1929–1945) was a German Jewish girl who wrote a diary while hiding for two years in a secret room in Amsterdam as she and her family tried to avoid the Nazi holocaust.

2. Source: Synopsis of research as reported in *Parade Magazine*, October 8, 2006.

3. Charles L. Allen (1913–2005) was a Georgia-born Methodist minister who served as pastor of Atlanta's Grace United Methodist Church (1948–1960), during which time Grace became the largest Methodist church in Georgia. In 1960, Allen moved to Houston, Texas to pastor the First United Methodist Church. During his tenure, it became the largest Methodist church in the world. This illustration is from his book, *The Twenty-Third Psalm, An Interpretation* (Westwood, NJ: Fleming H. Revell Company, 1961) pp. 11–13.

4. Sir Michael Faraday (1791–1867), the 19th century British scientist (physicist and chemist) contributed significantly to the fields of electromagnetism and electrochemistry and invented the earliest form of the device that would become the Bunsen burner. This quote is from a paper titled *Scientists and Their Gods* by Dr. Henry F. Schaefer, III, as published on the *Institute for Religious Research* website. See www.irr.org.

5. Warner Brothers' 2000 movie *Pay It Forward*, starring Kevin Spacey and Helen Hunt was adapted from the national best-selling novel *Pay It Forward* by Catherine Ryan Hyde.

Learn to Live!

1. Dale Carnegie (1888–1955), American author of *How to Win Friends and Influence People* and a biography of Abraham Lincoln titled *Lincoln the Unknown*. Mr. Carnegie was a pioneer in self-improvement, salesmanship. and corporate training programs.

2. Søren Kierkegaard (1813–1855) was a 19th century Danish philosopher, theologian and author.

About the Author

Carl's business management career began as a communications specialist in the United States Navy. Following an eight year Naval career, Carl enjoyed twenty-four years with the American Telephone and Telegraph Company, AT&T, where he held positions ranging from Communications Technician to District Manager.

Following an early retirement from AT&T, Carl founded, developed, and sold a mortgage brokerage company, established a residential lending department for a privately owned bank, and was Vice President–Operations for A&A Services, Inc., a national personnel staffing company.

Throughout his business career, Carl's passion has been to help people understand the importance of personal values and principles for achieving the best possible life—by any standard of measurement.

Upon his retirement from A&A Services in 2003, Carl founded Best Quest, Inc. and specializes in management consulting and facilitating workshops focused on personal development, ethics, leadership skills, and effective communication techniques.

Additionally, Carl established and served on the Board of Directors for the Educational Alliance Fund, a private non-profit foundation dedicated to strengthening America through education.

Carl and Martha live in Loganville, GA and have two children and six grandchildren.

CPSIA information can be obtained at www.ICGtesting.com
Printed in the USA
BVOW03s1811101214

378819BV00003B/20/P